Eat Great Food

_____

_____

_____

 Table of Contents

Page #	Recipe Name	Type	Date

Table of Contents

Page #	Recipe Name	Type	Date

Recipe Name:
_____
_____

Date: _____
Type: _____
Difficulty: 1 2 3 4 5 6 7 8 9 10

Serves:
_____

Prep Time:
_____

Cook Time:
_____

Oven Temp:
_____

Notes:
_____
_____
_____
_____
_____

Ingredients:

Directions:

Directions continued:

_____
_____
_____
_____
_____
_____
_____
_____
_____
_____
_____

Photos & Notes:

Recipe Name:

Date: _____
Type: _____
Difficulty: 1 2 3 4 5 6 7 8 9 10

Serves:
_____
Prep Time:
_____

Cook Time:
_____
Oven Temp:
_____

Notes:

Ingredients:

Directions:

Directions continued:

_____
_____
_____
_____
_____
_____
_____
_____
_____
_____
_____
_____

Photos & Notes:

Recipe Name:

Date: _____
Type: _____
Difficulty: 1 2 3 4 5 6 7 8 9 10

Serves: _____

Prep Time: _____

Cook Time: _____

Oven Temp: _____

Notes:

Ingredients:

Directions:

11

Directions continued:

Photos & Notes:

Recipe Name:

Date: _____
Type: _____
Difficulty: 1 2 3 4 5 6 7 8 9 10

Serves:
_____
Prep Time:
_____

Cook Time:
_____
Oven Temp:
_____

Notes:

Ingredients:

Directions:

Directions continued:

_____
_____
_____
_____
_____
_____
_____
_____
_____
_____

Photos & Notes:

Recipe Name:
_____
_____

Date: _____
Type: _____
Difficulty: 1 2 3 4 5 6 7 8 9 10

Serves:
_____

Prep Time:
_____

Cook Time:
_____

Oven Temp:
_____

Notes:
_____
_____
_____
_____
_____

Ingredients:

Directions:

15

Directions continued:

Photos & Notes:

Recipe Name:
_____
_____

Date: _____
Type: _____
Difficulty: 1 2 3 4 5 6 7 8 9 10

Serves:
_____

Prep Time:
_____

Cook Time:
_____

Oven Temp:
_____

Notes:
_____
_____
_____
_____
_____
_____

Ingredients:

Directions:

Directions continued:

_____
_____
_____
_____
_____
_____
_____
_____
_____
_____
_____
_____

Photos & Notes:

Recipe Name:

Date: _____
Type: _____
Difficulty: 1 2 3 4 5 6 7 8 9 10

Serves:
_____
Prep Time:
_____

Cook Time:
_____
Oven Temp:
_____

Notes:

Ingredients:

Directions:

Directions continued:

Photos & Notes:

Recipe Name:
_____
_____

Date: _____
Type: _____
Difficulty: 1 2 3 4 5 6 7 8 9 10

Serves:
_____
Prep Time:
_____

Cook Time:
_____
Oven Temp:
_____

Notes:
_____
_____
_____
_____
_____

Ingredients:

_____
_____
_____
_____
_____
_____
_____
_____
_____

Directions:

_____
_____
_____
_____
_____
_____
_____
_____
_____

Directions continued:

___

Photos & Notes:

Recipe Name:
_____
_____

Date: _____
Type: _____
Difficulty: 1 2 3 4 5 6 7 8 9 10

Serves:
_____

Prep Time:
_____

Cook Time:
_____

Oven Temp:
_____

Notes:
_____
_____
_____
_____
_____

Ingredients:
_____
_____
_____
_____
_____
_____
_____
_____
_____

Directions:
_____
_____
_____
_____
_____
_____
_____
_____
_____

Directions continued:

Photos & Notes:

Recipe Name:

Date:
Type:
Difficulty: 1 2 3 4 5 6 7 8 9 10

Serves:

Prep Time:

Cook Time:

Oven Temp:

Notes:

Ingredients:

Directions:

25

Directions continued:

_____
_____
_____
_____
_____
_____
_____
_____
_____
_____

Photos & Notes:

Recipe Name:
_____
_____

Date: _____
Type: _____
Difficulty: 1 2 3 4 5 6 7 8 9 10

Serves:
_____

Prep Time:
_____

Cook Time:
_____

Oven Temp:
_____

Notes:
_____
_____
_____
_____
_____

Ingredients:

_____
_____
_____
_____
_____
_____
_____
_____
_____
_____

Directions:

_____
_____
_____
_____
_____
_____
_____
_____
_____
_____

Directions continued:

_____
_____
_____
_____
_____
_____
_____
_____
_____
_____
_____
_____
_____

Photos & Notes:

Recipe Name:
_____
_____

Date: _____
Type: _____
Difficulty: 1 2 3 4 5 6 7 8 9 10

Serves:
_____

Prep Time:
_____

Cook Time:
_____

Oven Temp:
_____

Notes:
_____
_____
_____
_____
_____
_____

Ingredients:

Directions:

Directions continued:

_____
_____
_____
_____
_____
_____
_____
_____
_____
_____

Photos & Notes:

Recipe Name:
_____
_____

Date: _____
Type: _____
Difficulty: 1 2 3 4 5 6 7 8 9 10

Serves:
_____

Prep Time:
_____

Cook Time:
_____

Oven Temp:
_____

Notes:
_____
_____
_____
_____
_____

Ingredients:
_____
_____
_____
_____
_____
_____
_____
_____
_____

Directions:
_____
_____
_____
_____
_____
_____
_____
_____
_____

Directions continued:

___

Photos & Notes:

Recipe Name:

Date: _____
Type: _____
Difficulty: 1 2 3 4 5 6 7 8 9 10

Serves: _____

Prep Time: _____

Cook Time: _____

Oven Temp: _____

Notes:

Ingredients:

Directions:

Directions continued:

_____
_____
_____
_____
_____
_____
_____
_____
_____
_____
_____
_____

Photos & Notes:

Recipe Name:

Date: _____
Type: _____
Difficulty: 1 2 3 4 5 6 7 8 9 10

Serves:

Prep Time:

Cook Time:

Oven Temp:

Notes:

Ingredients:

Directions:

35

Directions continued:

_____
_____
_____
_____
_____
_____
_____
_____
_____
_____
_____
_____
_____

Photos & Notes:

Recipe Name:
_____
_____

Date: _____
Type: _____
Difficulty: 1 2 3 4 5 6 7 8 9 10

Serves:
_____

Prep Time:
_____

Cook Time:
_____

Oven Temp:
_____

Notes:
_____
_____
_____
_____
_____
_____

Ingredients:

_____
_____
_____
_____
_____
_____
_____
_____
_____
_____

Directions:

_____
_____
_____
_____
_____
_____
_____
_____
_____
_____

Directions continued:

Photos & Notes:

Recipe Name:
_____
_____

Date: _____
Type: _____
Difficulty: 1 2 3 4 5 6 7 8 9 10

Serves:
_____
Prep Time:
_____

Cook Time:
_____
Oven Temp:
_____

Notes:
_____
_____
_____
_____
_____
_____

Ingredients:

_____
_____
_____
_____
_____
_____
_____
_____
_____
_____

Directions:

_____
_____
_____
_____
_____
_____
_____
_____
_____
_____

Directions continued:

_____
_____
_____
_____
_____
_____
_____
_____
_____
_____
_____
_____

Photos & Notes:

Recipe Name:

Date: _____
Type: _____
Difficulty: 1 2 3 4 5 6 7 8 9 10

Serves:
_____

Prep Time:
_____

Cook Time:
_____

Oven Temp:
_____

Notes:

Ingredients:

Directions:

Directions continued:

_____
_____
_____
_____
_____
_____
_____
_____
_____
_____
_____
_____
_____

Photos & Notes:

Recipe Name:
_____
_____

Date: _____
Type: _____
Difficulty: 1 2 3 4 5 6 7 8 9 10

Serves:
_____

Prep Time:
_____

Cook Time:
_____

Oven Temp:
_____

Notes:
_____
_____
_____
_____
_____

Ingredients:
_____
_____
_____
_____
_____
_____
_____
_____
_____
_____

Directions:
_____
_____
_____
_____
_____
_____
_____
_____
_____
_____

Directions continued:

_____
_____
_____
_____
_____
_____
_____
_____
_____
_____
_____
_____

Photos & Notes:

Recipe Name:
_____
_____

Date: _____
Type: _____
Difficulty: 1 2 3 4 5 6 7 8 9 10

Serves:
_____

Prep Time:
_____

Cook Time:
_____

Oven Temp:
_____

Notes:
_____
_____
_____
_____
_____
_____

Ingredients:

Directions:

Directions continued:

Photos & Notes:

Recipe Name:
_____
_____

Date: _____
Type: _____
Difficulty: 1 2 3 4 5 6 7 8 9 10

Serves:
_____
Prep Time:
_____

Cook Time:
_____
Oven Temp:
_____

Notes:
_____
_____
_____
_____
_____

Ingredients:
_____
_____
_____
_____
_____
_____
_____
_____
_____

Directions:
_____
_____
_____
_____
_____
_____
_____
_____
_____

Directions continued:

Photos & Notes:

Recipe Name:
_____
_____

Date: _____
Type: _____
Difficulty: 1 2 3 4 5 6 7 8 9 10

Serves:
_____

Prep Time:
_____

Cook Time:
_____

Oven Temp:
_____

Notes:
_____
_____
_____
_____
_____

Ingredients:

Directions:

Directions continued:

_____
_____
_____
_____
_____
_____
_____
_____
_____
_____
_____

Photos & Notes:

Recipe Name:
_____
_____

Date: _____
Type: _____
Difficulty: 1 2 3 4 5 6 7 8 9 10

Serves:
_____

Prep Time:
_____

Cook Time:
_____

Oven Temp:
_____

Notes:
_____
_____
_____
_____
_____

Ingredients:

_____
_____
_____
_____
_____
_____
_____
_____
_____

Directions:

_____
_____
_____
_____
_____
_____
_____
_____
_____

Directions continued:

Photos & Notes:

Recipe Name:
_____
_____

Date: _____
Type: _____
Difficulty: 1 2 3 4 5 6 7 8 9 10

Serves:
_____

Prep Time:
_____

Cook Time:
_____

Oven Temp:
_____

Notes:
_____
_____
_____
_____
_____

Ingredients:

Directions:

Directions continued:

Photos & Notes:

Recipe Name:
_____
_____

Date: _____
Type: _____
Difficulty: 1 2 3 4 5 6 7 8 9 10

Serves:
_____

Prep Time:
_____

Cook Time:
_____

Oven Temp:
_____

Notes:
_____
_____
_____
_____
_____

Ingredients:

Directions:

Directions continued:

Photos & Notes:

Recipe Name:
_____
_____

Date: _____
Type: _____
Difficulty: 1 2 3 4 5 6 7 8 9 10

Serves:
_____

Prep Time:
_____

Cook Time:
_____

Oven Temp:
_____

Notes:
_____
_____
_____
_____
_____
_____

Ingredients:

Directions:

Directions continued:

Photos & Notes:

Recipe Name:
_____
_____

Date: _____
Type: _____
Difficulty: 1 2 3 4 5 6 7 8 9 10

Serves:
_____

Prep Time:
_____

Cook Time:
_____

Oven Temp:
_____

Notes:
_____
_____
_____
_____
_____

Ingredients:

Directions:

Directions continued:

Photos & Notes:

Recipe Name:
_____
_____

Date: _____
Type: _____
Difficulty: 1 2 3 4 5 6 7 8 9 10

Serves:
_____
Prep Time:
_____

Cook Time:
_____
Oven Temp:
_____

Notes:
_____
_____
_____
_____
_____

Ingredients:

_____
_____
_____
_____
_____
_____
_____
_____
_____

Directions:

_____
_____
_____
_____
_____
_____
_____
_____
_____

Directions continued:

Photos & Notes:

Recipe Name:
_____
_____

Date: _____
Type: _____
Difficulty: 1 2 3 4 5 6 7 8 9 10

Serves:
_____
Prep Time:
_____

Cook Time:
_____
Oven Temp:
_____

Notes:
_____
_____
_____
_____
_____

Ingredients:

Directions:

Directions continued:

_____
_____
_____
_____
_____
_____
_____
_____
_____
_____
_____
_____

Photos & Notes:

Recipe Name:
_____
_____

Date: _____
Type: _____
Difficulty: 1 2 3 4 5 6 7 8 9 10

Serves:
_____

Prep Time:
_____

Cook Time:
_____

Oven Temp:
_____

Notes:
_____
_____
_____
_____
_____

Ingredients:

Directions:

Directions continued:

Photos & Notes:

Recipe Name:
_____
_____

Date: _____
Type: _____
Difficulty: 1 2 3 4 5 6 7 8 9 10

Serves:
_____

Prep Time:
_____

Cook Time:
_____

Oven Temp:
_____

Notes:
_____
_____
_____
_____
_____

Ingredients:

_____
_____
_____
_____
_____
_____
_____
_____
_____

Directions:

_____
_____
_____
_____
_____
_____
_____
_____
_____

Directions continued:

Photos & Notes:

Recipe Name:

Date: _____
Type: _____
Difficulty: 1 2 3 4 5 6 7 8 9 10

Serves:
_____
Prep Time:
_____

Cook Time:
_____
Oven Temp:
_____

Notes:

Ingredients:

Directions:

Directions continued:

_____
_____
_____
_____
_____
_____
_____
_____
_____
_____
_____

Photos & Notes:

Recipe Name:
_____
_____

Date: _____
Type: _____
Difficulty: 1 2 3 4 5 6 7 8 9 10

Serves:
_____

Prep Time:
_____

Cook Time:
_____

Oven Temp:
_____

Notes:
_____
_____
_____
_____
_____
_____

Ingredients:

Directions:

Directions continued:

Photos & Notes:

Recipe Name:

Date: _____
Type: _____
Difficulty: 1 2 3 4 5 6 7 8 9 10

Serves:
_____
Prep Time:
_____

Cook Time:
_____
Oven Temp:
_____

Notes:

Ingredients:

Directions:

Directions continued:

Photos & Notes:

Recipe Name:
_____
_____

Date: _____
Type: _____
Difficulty: 1 2 3 4 5 6 7 8 9 10

Serves:
_____

Prep Time:
_____

Cook Time:
_____

Oven Temp:
_____

Notes:
_____
_____
_____
_____
_____

Ingredients:

_____
_____
_____
_____
_____
_____
_____
_____
_____
_____

Directions:

_____
_____
_____
_____
_____
_____
_____
_____
_____
_____

Directions continued:

Photos & Notes:

Recipe Name:
_____
_____

Date: _____
Type: _____
Difficulty: 1 2 3 4 5 6 7 8 9 10

Serves:
_____

Prep Time:
_____

Cook Time:
_____

Oven Temp:
_____

Notes:
_____
_____
_____
_____
_____

Ingredients:

Directions:

Directions continued:

___

Photos & Notes:

Recipe Name:
_____
_____

Date: _____
Type: _____
Difficulty: 1 2 3 4 5 6 7 8 9 10

Serves:
_____
Prep Time:
_____

Cook Time:
_____
Oven Temp:
_____

Notes:
_____
_____
_____
_____

Ingredients:

Directions:

Directions continued:

Photos & Notes:

Recipe Name:

Date: _____
Type: _____
Difficulty: 1 2 3 4 5 6 7 8 9 10

Serves: _____

Prep Time: _____

Cook Time: _____

Oven Temp: _____

Notes:
_____
_____
_____
_____
_____

Ingredients:

Directions:

Directions continued:

Photos & Notes:

Recipe Name:
_____
_____

Date: _____
Type: _____
Difficulty: 1 2 3 4 5 6 7 8 9 10

Serves:
_____

Prep Time:
_____

Cook Time:
_____

Oven Temp:
_____

Notes:
_____
_____
_____
_____
_____

Ingredients:

Directions:

Directions continued:

_____

Photos & Notes:

Recipe Name:
_____
_____

Date: _____
Type: _____
Difficulty: 1 2 3 4 5 6 7 8 9 10

Serves:
_____

Prep Time:
_____

Cook Time:
_____

Oven Temp:
_____

Notes:
_____
_____
_____
_____
_____

Ingredients:

Directions:

Directions continued:

Photos & Notes:

Recipe Name:
_____
_____

Date: _____
Type: _____
Difficulty: 1 2 3 4 5 6 7 8 9 10

Serves:
_____

Prep Time:
_____

Cook Time:
_____

Oven Temp:
_____

Notes:
_____
_____
_____
_____
_____
_____

Ingredients:

Directions:

Directions continued:

_____
_____
_____
_____
_____
_____
_____
_____
_____
_____
_____
_____

Photos & Notes:

Recipe Name:
_____
_____

Date: _____
Type: _____
Difficulty: 1 2 3 4 5 6 7 8 9 10

Serves:
_____

Prep Time:
_____

Cook Time:
_____

Oven Temp:
_____

Notes:
_____
_____
_____
_____
_____

Ingredients:

Directions:

Directions continued:

_____
_____
_____
_____
_____
_____
_____
_____
_____
_____
_____

Photos & Notes:

Recipe Name:
_____
_____

Date: _____
Type: _____
Difficulty: 1 2 3 4 5 6 7 8 9 10

Serves:
_____

Prep Time:
_____

Cook Time:
_____

Oven Temp:
_____

Notes:
_____
_____
_____
_____
_____

Ingredients:

Directions:

Directions continued:

Photos & Notes:

Recipe Name:
_____
_____

Date: _____
Type: _____
Difficulty: 1 2 3 4 5 6 7 8 9 10

Serves:
_____

Prep Time:
_____

Cook Time:
_____

Oven Temp:
_____

Notes:
_____
_____
_____
_____
_____

Ingredients:

Directions:

Directions continued:

Photos & Notes:

Recipe Name:
_____
_____

Date: _____
Type: _____
Difficulty: 1 2 3 4 5 6 7 8 9 10

Serves:
_____

Prep Time:
_____

Cook Time:
_____

Oven Temp:
_____

Notes:
_____
_____
_____
_____
_____
_____

Ingredients:

Directions:

Directions continued:

Photos & Notes:

Recipe Name:

Date:
Type:
Difficulty: 1 2 3 4 5 6 7 8 9 10

Serves:

Prep Time:

Cook Time:

Oven Temp:

Notes:

Ingredients:

Directions:

Directions continued:

Photos & Notes:

Recipe Name:
_____
_____

Date: _____
Type: _____
Difficulty: 1 2 3 4 5 6 7 8 9 10

Serves:
_____

Prep Time:
_____

Cook Time:
_____

Oven Temp:
_____

Notes:
_____
_____
_____
_____
_____

Ingredients:

Directions:

Directions continued:

_____
_____
_____
_____
_____
_____
_____
_____
_____
_____
_____
_____

Photos & Notes:

Recipe Name:
_____
_____

Date: _____
Type: _____
Difficulty: 1 2 3 4 5 6 7 8 9 10

Serves:
_____
Prep Time:
_____

Cook Time:
_____
Oven Temp:
_____

Notes:
_____
_____
_____
_____
_____

Ingredients:

Directions:

101

Directions continued:

Photos & Notes:

Recipe Name:
_____
_____

Date: _____
Type: _____
Difficulty: 1 2 3 4 5 6 7 8 9 10

Serves:
_____

Prep Time:
_____

Cook Time:
_____

Oven Temp:
_____

Notes:
_____
_____
_____
_____
_____

Ingredients:
_____
_____
_____
_____
_____
_____
_____
_____

Directions:
_____
_____
_____
_____
_____
_____
_____
_____

Directions continued:

Photos & Notes:

Recipe Name:
_____
_____

Date: _____
Type: _____
Difficulty: 1 2 3 4 5 6 7 8 9 10

Serves:
_____

Prep Time:
_____

Cook Time:
_____

Oven Temp:
_____

Notes:
_____
_____
_____
_____
_____
_____

Ingredients:

Directions:

105

Directions continued:

Photos & Notes:

Recipe Name:
_____
_____

Date: _____
Type: _____
Difficulty: 1 2 3 4 5 6 7 8 9 10

Serves:
_____

Prep Time:
_____

Cook Time:
_____

Oven Temp:
_____

Notes:
_____
_____
_____
_____
_____
_____

Ingredients:

Directions:

Directions continued:

_____
_____
_____
_____
_____
_____
_____
_____
_____
_____

Photos & Notes:

Recipe Name:
_____
_____

Date: _____
Type: _____
Difficulty: 1 2 3 4 5 6 7 8 9 10

Serves:
_____

Prep Time:
_____

Cook Time:
_____

Oven Temp:
_____

Notes:
_____
_____
_____
_____
_____

Ingredients:

Directions:

Directions continued:

Photos & Notes:

Made in United States
Troutdale, OR
12/08/2024

25988457R00064